# Cosmic
## ANSWERS

VII
CHARIOT.

**Cosmic Answers**
First published in 2019

© Adrian Everitt 2019
The moral rights of the author have been asserted.

All rights reserved. Except as permitted under
the Australian Copyright Act 1968 (for example, a
fair dealing for the purposes of study, research,
criticism or review), no part of this book may
be reproduced, stored in a retrieval system,
communicated or transmitted in any form or by
any means without prior written permission.

Title: *Cosmic Answers*
Creator: Adrian Everitt (author)
ISBN: 978-0-6485415-9-2

# Cosmic ANSWERS

Adrian Everitt

# Contents

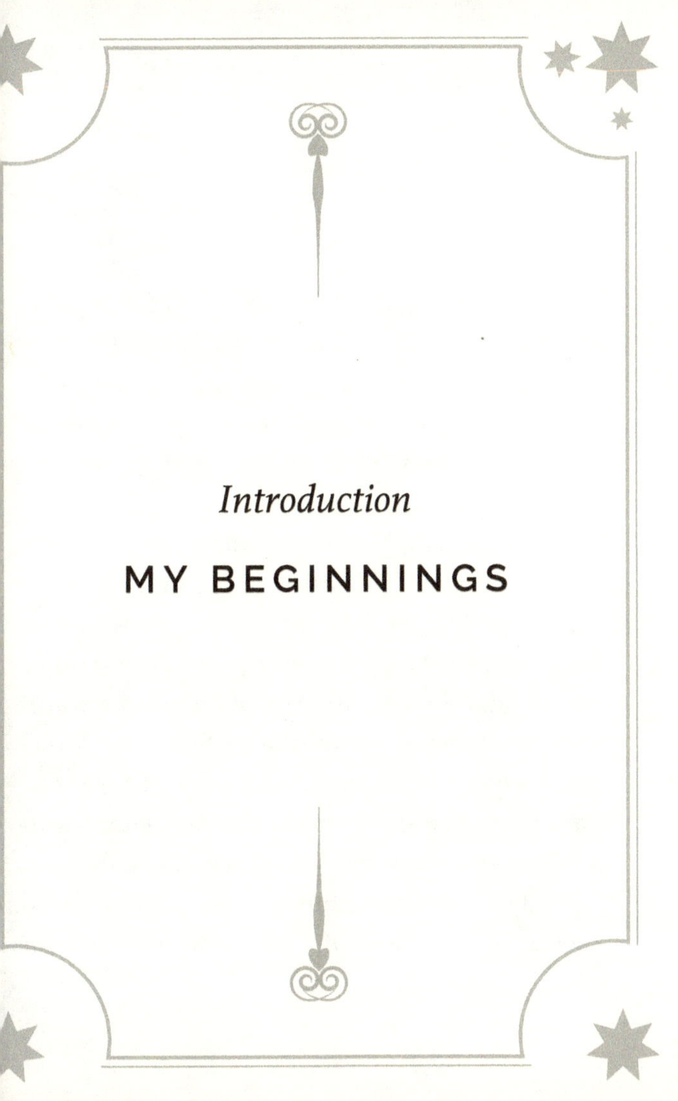

*Introduction*

# MY BEGINNINGS

From a young age I have experienced the para-normal, spiritual coincidences and synchronici-ties. Now at the age of 34, I am writing this book to tell you about my experiences, what's led to where I am today, and this journey that I am on.

I'm clairsentient, but would rather say I am an intuitive psychic, a phrase I learned about a while ago. I never seemed to fit in anywhere. I didn't belong to a certain group or type at school, but blended in with all sorts of people. I always knew there was something different or "odd" about myself, but I could not work out what it was. Then one day I saw a fortune teller for a reading, and I was told I am spiritually gifted. At first I didn't believe it, but over time it started to make sense, as you shall find out when you start reading the following chapters!

I have an intuitive sense of knowing about things, and I can't stand being around negativity as I am empathic. This means that watching TV can be maddeningly overwhelming for me, and I have cried during many movies or documentaries. At times I wake up every night because I've had vivid prophetic dreams, in which I receive spiritual information, or I am visited by my spirit guides. I have experienced dreams like this all my life, but wasn't been able to figure it out until just a few years ago.

Things happening as coincidences or synchronicities seem to play a big role in my life. These can be experienced as something to grab my attention, something that seems as if it was meant to be for me, or something that wasn't meant to happen to me - in which case I would be pushed in another direction.

These are just a few of the things that happen because of my spiritual gift. There are many more things too.

For some time I have offered fortune telling with Tarot or Oracle Cards, regardless of whether I have been working full time, part time, or on a casual basis. It has just developed as a part of who I am, and it feels as if I'm destined to do it. At times it has been a struggle to persist with tarot and oracle reading using my spiritual abilities. However, I still keep trying to gain more clients and retain existing clients, and I continue to practise readings and many other spiritual practices whilst I'm earning a living by other means.

Please enjoy my book. I hope you find it fascinating to read these short stories about my life and how I got to where I am today.

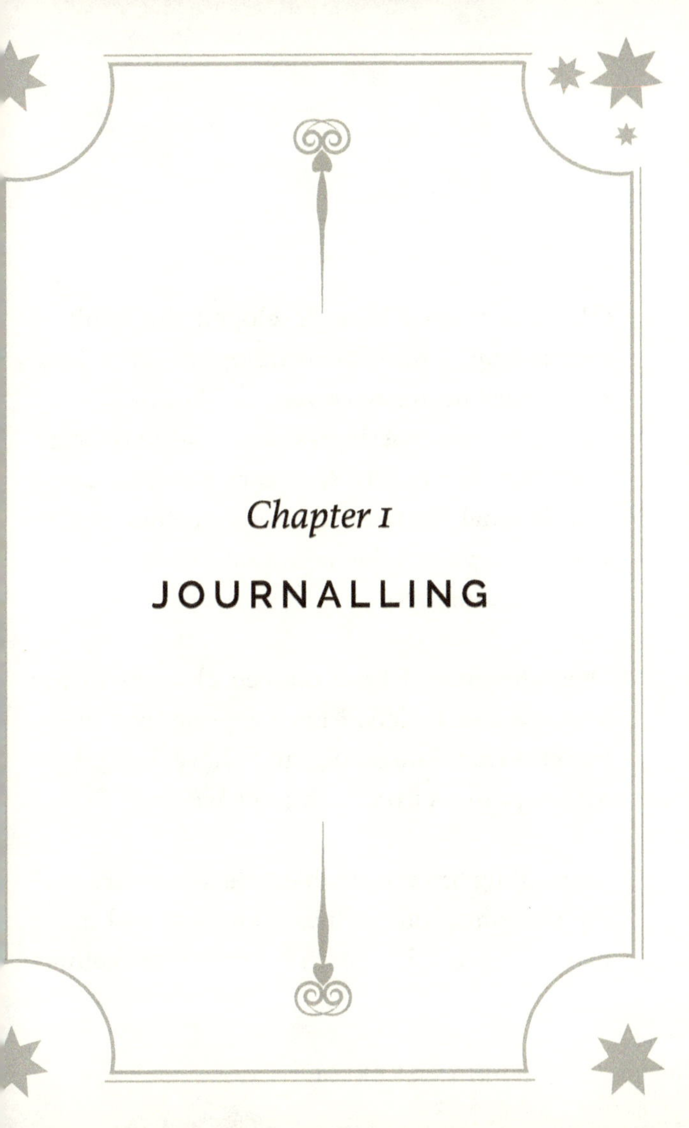

# Chapter 1

# JOURNALLING

Over the years I have developed the habit of journalling. I have been doing so for a long time and I'm pretty certain the hobby started during a period of depression. I have now kept a journal for nearly six years straight. Every new journal has been a different colour or size, which is a part of the habit that makes my journalling more unique.

Over the years I have noticed changes in my attitude and beliefs. I have experienced many benefits from journaling, and I have derived joy and happiness from within my writing.

Journalling has also enabled me to keep track of my thoughts and feelings, moments and memories. I've seen changes in my thoughts, feelings and outlook on things, and I can also have a laugh at myself from some of words I've written.

As well as writing in my journal, I have been cutting and pasting bits and pieces into it, such as movie tickets or my horoscope for the week. This helps me to keep track of many of the things in my life.

In my journals are all the positives and the good things I have found within each day. No matter how bad my bad was, I have always tried to find something positive from every day.

Journalling is what you make of it. It can be great fun - once I started I haven't wanted to stop!

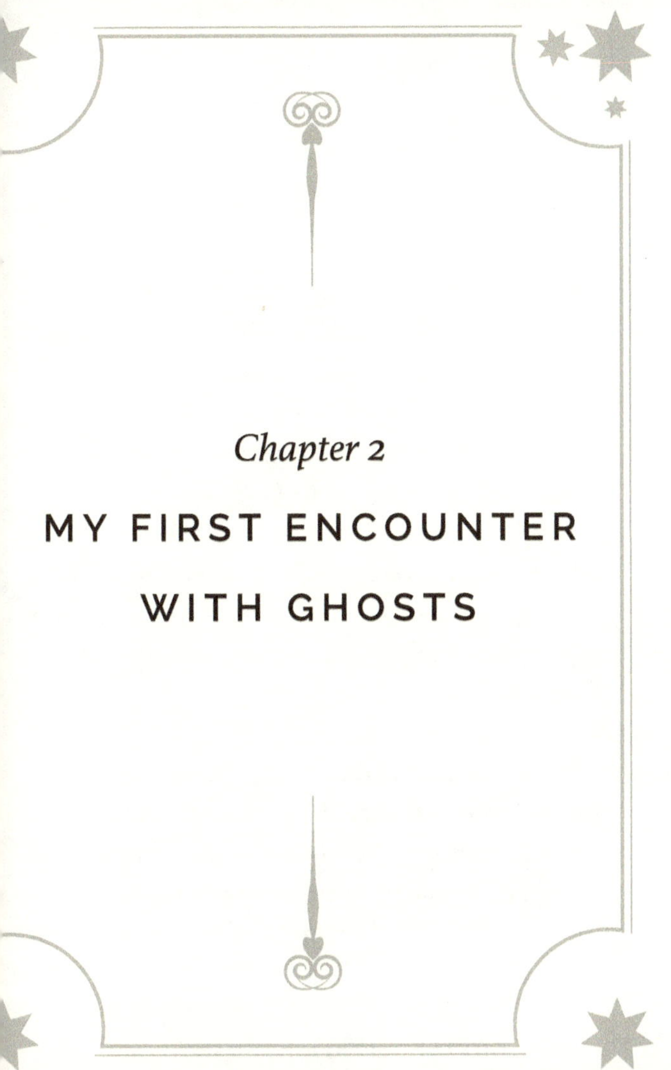

*Chapter 2*

# MY FIRST ENCOUNTER WITH GHOSTS

I first encountered ghosts when I was five years old and living at home with my mum, dad, older brother and younger brother.

We lived in an old weatherboard house with a tin roof, and front and back verandahs. The house was painted white all around, and had a white fence. There was an orange gravel drive-way right down to the back of the house. It also had a really big backyard and an outdoor laundry.

This is my first memory of "home" and what home meant to me. When my mum and dad moved in they didn't know the house was haunted; it wasn't until some time later that Mum and my brothers noticed spiritual activity within it.

     ADRIAN EVERITT

The house had two bedrooms. I slept in the second bedroom, sometimes with my older brother, but sometimes I didn't share the bedroom. Whenever I spent time sleeping alone in this room, I experienced spiritual activity.

My bed was placed in the top right corner of the room near the window on the left, and the door was at the foot of my bed, slightly to the left. The window looked out onto the fence and the neighbour's house. There wasn't much of a view.

At night I would go to sleep, then after a couple of hours - sometimes a few - I would feel my bed moving, and rising up from the floor. I still remember seeing it lift up, and moving me with it. I now know that it was a ghost. Sometimes it lifted my bed up and down again repeatedly, and at other times it would lift up my bed and spin it around the room really fast - with me still on it.

This was a scary experience for a five-year-old. Occasionally I would cry and scream for help, and the ghost would place the bed back where it should be. Then after a while it would move it again, or it would pick me up then leave me alone. At this age I didn't know or understand what was going on or happening.

Sometimes my older brother wouldn't be in the room with me because he'd be sleeping in the same room as Mum, and his bed would be empty. So there were nights when the ghost would lift up my bed, shift it across to the other side of the room, and place it alongside my brother's bed, making our two beds into a kind of double bed. I would crawl across to my brother's bed to escape, thinking that would make a difference.

At times I recall Mum coming to see what I was screaming about because she could hear me yelling and freaking out. But by the time she came into my room, the spiritual activity would usually have calmed down or stopped. And then it might start again as soon as Mum left the room or shut my bedroom door.

     ADRIAN EVERITT

Another thing that happened was when I saw two lights in the room where I slept. I would describe them as "car headlights" or "car lights", but there was no way a car could drive into the room or even flash its headlights in, because the neighbour's house was right alongside our house. The only explanation could be that it was spiritual activity.

As I was lying asleep in bed at night, the room would light up and glow for a while, and the two lights would flash around the walls of the room, darting back and forth. This experience was disturbing, but less frightening than when my bed was moved. But it bothered me as I couldn't sleep when it was happening.

Mum used to be chased down the corridor by the ghosts in this house. Whenever it happened, she would scream and yell at them to go away. And my Nanna can remember seeing "the ghosts" crawling out the laundry window. Once my uncle stayed overnight to experience the spiritual activity in my bedroom. He still remembers the experience and how frightening it was.

But the spirits didn't bother my dad. He was a non-believer, and anyway he was often busy working in the night. Mum and I would talk to him about our experiences but Dad wouldn't believe us. This was the frustrating part of the experience – it would have been nice if he had believed what we told him.

There had been two deaths in the house, a father and a son. I can't remember why and how they passed away in the house, but I am sure this was the reason that we experienced spiritual activity there. And so it was my first ever experience of spiritual activity!

    ADRIAN EVERITT

*Chapter 3*

# THE FAMILY PET THAT SAVED ME

This event took place in 1997, when I was 12 years old and living with my family in a small town called Bunbury in Western Australia.

It was a hot summer's day and we went for a swim as a family with our pet dogs at the local beach. For a couple of hours we had all been swimming and throwing balls into the water for the dogs to play fetch.

It came to the point where my mum decided it was time to leave the beach and head home. She had been sitting on the beach whilst my brothers, stepdad and I, together with the dogs, went to swim and play further down the beach. Mum was looking after our belongings and supervising what was going on from where she sat.

     ADRIAN EVERITT

Because Mum had declared it was time to go, everyone else had left the water and started heading back up the beach, ready to walk on towards the car.

I was in the water making my way back to shore. I was a fair way out, and the water was up to my waist. Then one of our dogs ran from the water and I lost my balance. I fell backwards in the water, and went under. I started panicking and waving my arms around. I wasn't yelling loudly, but was saying "argh - argh".

It was enough noise for the dog called Nona to hear me, and she came to rescue me from the water, I remember feeling her nose nudging me towards to the shore. I also felt Nona's teeth in my soggy wet t-shirt, pulling me along.

At about this time I heard Mum yelling, "He's drowning!" Then I heard my stepdad saying, "Who?" before looking back to the beach and running into the water. At this very moment I took a glance towards the beach and saw him racing into the water to rescue me from drowning.

By the time my family packed the car and everybody got in, only to realise I was missing, it would have been too late. My drowning experience was happening that quickly! I can imagine them noticing that I was missing and wondering where I'd got to, searching up and down the beach and all around, looking for me, without realising I was drowning in the water.

The dog knocked me then pushed me down a sand bar into deeper water which caused me to drown. I was so lucky that the family dog Nona saved me. Otherwise I wouldn't be here today to tell the tale. We occasionally remind each other of the time I nearly drowned at the beach and how awesome was the dog that saved me.

We can't remember how the our family pet Nona was named as it was a long, long time ago. However, I have found that the name Nona comes from the Latin word meaning "ninth", and refers to the nine months of pregnancy; it was traditionally given to the ninth child in a family.

*Chapter 4*

# SOMETHING'S NOT RIGHT!

In 2002 I was living in Rockingham in Western Australia and had finished high school. I'd had a couple of jobs here and there, but then I fell out of employment. So I was signed up for the Work for the Dole program.

On this particular day I was on my way to the employment agency and the Work for the Dole op shop. My step dad was driving the family van and I was sitting in the passenger seat.

I was feeling agitated and reluctant to be going to Work for the Dole. We were talking about this, and in the conversation I made sure my voice was heard and my opinion was strong. My step dad said, "Just do it and see how you go."

I can remember saying how lucky some people

have it when they leave school, and then there's me going to this program. Some of my friends from high school were going to university or TAFE, or had a place of employment.

"They have it better than me," I was saying. "It's not fair! How things can be so unfair? Why can't I be like them?"

We arrived at the employment agency and Work for the Dole op shop 10 minutes early and waited for the building to open. After a short time, some employment agency workers arrived and allowed me to enter.

It was like any other day inside the office. There were phones ringing, smiling faces from the workers and receptionist, and positive outlooks, with everyone saying "Good morning" and "How are you?"

But as I was passing through the building, I still felt uneasy and apprehensive about being there.

In fact, I didn't want to be there at all. I wanted to run back out the door and go home again.

Everyone else's vibes and energies weren't matching my vibes and energies. At this stage I started getting an intuitive feeling that something just wasn't right, but I couldn't figure out what it was.

At 8 am, I was still feeling hypersensitive. Our Work for the Dole supervisor was having a chat with me and a young pregnant lady, about the day and what we would be doing in the op shop. We had discussed the safety procedures and fire safety drill and what we were to do if something was to happen. At this point I was still feeling that something was going to happen but had no idea what. The supervisor explained the procedure and reassured us that everything would be fine.

At 9 am it was time to open the op shop as usual. The young lady and I were sitting there having a small conversation about nothing in particular.

Time ticked on. It was 10 am, time for the morning tea break. The young lady and I went out of the shop to the back of the building to have a break. The supervisor manned the op shop while we were gone. We were back by 10:30 am.

Around then a strange young man came through the store. The young lady was sitting by the counter resting. I was on the floor of the shop, tinkering away doing some work. I was still feeling and thinking the same as I had all morning.

This young man come through the store, checking out everything we sold and stocked. The young lady behind the counter pulled faces at me and pointed to him.

His behaviour was suspicious. He didn't behave like a normal customer. He was interested and looking, but in a different way to the other customers, because he didn't display any interest in the products, or pick up and look at even a couple of things, or try on items of clothing.

At this time my thoughts and feelings had zoned in on this strange man wandering around the op shop and my intuition was strongly telling me there was something about this person. A couple of times I followed him because I felt intuitively compelled to, but the young lady behind the counter noticed and told me not to via hand signals.

The strange guy left the store. At around 11:30 am he returned. He came into the shop in a hurry, quickly glanced around the store and made his way to the front counter near the door. I moved behind the counter. At this stage, every-thing inside me was telling me something was going badly, something wasn't right!

The strange guy then put his right hand down into the jacket he was wearing, then lunged for-ward and grabbed the donation tin that was on the counter.

It was a fight or flight situation. We didn't know

whether he was armed with a knife or gun, or nothing at all and was just trying to give us a scare. At the same time, we couldn't be too careful in case we ended up being sorry for not trying to stop him.

It all happened so quickly. The young pregnant lady was leaning backwards in the chair, in the hope that he wasn't going to attack her.

Adrenaline was rushing through me. I knew that something was going to happen each time it did. Instinct and intuition, and a feeling about what to do next was already in my mind. I didn't know where all this information came from, but it was in my mind and I listened to it.

I raced out of the op shop after the strange guy who had taken the donation tin. He had turned right and was running down the street. I raced back inside, through the shop, then opened the door into the waiting and reception area of the employment agency. Without thinking I told the receptionist that we'd had an emergency and been held up. Next thing the building was shut down and the front door to the agency was locked. The office staff in the employment agency behind the shop were all told the situation and they started leaving.

It was the longest 30 minutes, but by midday the police were searching the area for this person.

The police took me into an office and interviewed me about the occurrence and then did the same with the young lady who had been with me. Then my family were called and I went home.

It was a big experience for me to have been so tuned in to my intuition and inner guidance, and to have experienced clairsentience throughout the day.

*Chapter 5*

# DRIVING THROUGH KAPUNDA

When I was around 14 or 15 years old, we went on a family holiday around Australia with our caravan and family van. We lived in Western Australia at the time, so we started there and made our way across to South Australia.

I remember my Mum and stepdad having conversations, talking about where to go next. They exchanged ideas, opinions and thoughts, and then we started heading towards Kapunda. The reason for going there was because they had seen this place featured on a TV documentary about hauntings and haunted towns. Back at this time Kapunda was the most haunted town in Australia, although it may not be now.

We drove towards Kapunda in South Australia, and some kilometres away from the town I started to feel uneasy, as if going to this town wasn't a good idea. I was feeling faint and cold, the way you feel cold when you have a temperature. I wanted rugs and blankets to keep myself warm. I hadn't felt like this even an hour ago. As we drove along, I felt as if I was retrieving information and sensing parts of my surroundings, such as buildings, places, houses and environments.

I seemed to be experiencing clairsentience, or clear feeling. This is the ability to feel strongly and to sense the emotions and feelings of the people, places, animals and spirits that are around you. I didn't realise this at the time. Back then I didn't have a clue what clairsentience was.

As we neared Kapunda I started looking out the window all around the car, because I had begun to notice spiritual activity and ghosts around Kapunda. I saw spirits moving around the cemetery during daylight, and I saw spirits walking down the street. This just freaked me out. I felt a headache coming on rapidly.

We drove along Clare Road and stopped at an intersection where there was a big old building with a veranda. It was the North Kapunda Hotel. This is where I felt really unwell; I felt so sick that I wanted to vomit badly, although fortunately that never happened. This urge to be sick came out of nowhere and hit me suddenly. The urge to vomit was so strong as we were sitting in the car at the intersection, and I couldn't believe I was feeling like this. I saw spirits - shadowy figures wandering around inside. I remember seeing a couple of spirits outside too. One spirit was sitting down at a table, and I couldn't help fixing my attention on it every now and then while we waited at the intersection.

I was whingeing to my mum all the time and she was becoming agitated and annoyed with me. I was complaining: "Can we get out of here, because I don't feel so good. I'm going to vomit and my head is so sore."

I looked out the car window and saw ghosts inside the old building, on the second storey and ground level. Some even floated right up towards the car quickly and back again, which really freaked me out.

I can still recall vividly seeing a cat running down the street to a house. I remember saying to everybody in the van, "Look out the for cat!" But they just said, "Where is it?" They couldn't see it. But I certainly saw it running down the street to a house, sitting outside at the front near a fence, then jumping over it and disappearing.

I was frustrated by this and I reminded them all that we were in a haunted town and there would be strange things happening around here. Fortunately, we never got out of the van at Kapunda. We were just passing through and checking it out. After we had driven a short distance out of the town, everything that was wrong with me started to ease and I felt better.

Since writing this book in 2017, I have done some internet searches on Kapunda and found out that Kapunda is the most haunted town in Australia, and that there was a murder in the North Kapunda Hotel.

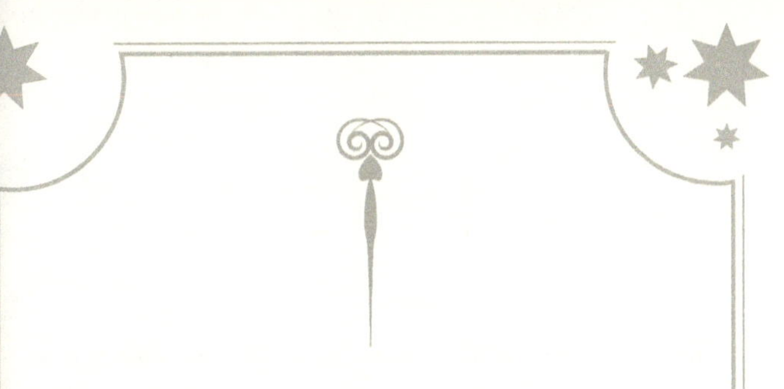

*Chapter 6*

# CHRISTMAS WITHOUT

# MY FAMILY

This chapter isn't exactly spiritual in the sense that it is not about clairvoyance and psychic abilities, but hopefully you'll soon understand what it is about. I hope you enjoy reading it.

One year when I was in about twenty or twenty-one years old, I spent Christmas Day without my family. I spent it all by myself.

I tried to find ways to make it over to Perth to be with my family at Christmas time, but it just wasn't possible since I was unemployed and didn't have the funds to get there and back.

I was living in Melbourne, in a shared house with older people and I was unable to spend the day with them. One of my housemates had invited me to come and join her family for Christmas, but I declined the offer.

On Christmas morning I woke early. The house was rather eerily quiet. There was not a sound apart from the hum of the fridge in the kitchen. I woke and lay in bed for a little while, thinking, and encouraging myself to get up, get dressed and go out.

So I did. I went to the bathroom and came back with some nice clothes on, went to the kitchen and made breakfast, the same old usual breakfast, nothing special. Time ticked on and I was ready to go to church for the Christmas Day service. A knock at the door alerted me that it was time to go. I was nervous, as I had never thought I'd do something like this, and at the time I had no idea what to expect; so my companion gave me a rough idea of how the day was going to be.

The church was a Pentecostal Christian church.

I wasn't much of a church person or even religious at this time. When we arrived the place was packed with churchgoers. I jumped out of the bus and went inside with the group I was with, and was ushered over to a table where I would be sitting for a while.

I was a stranger at my table. Everybody else knew each other, and were chatting amongst themselves. Every now and then they would realise I was there and have a quick chat with me.

The place was abuzz, full of positive energy and excitement. Nearly all the people there knew each other, I realised. I didn't know anybody expect the acquaintances I had made on the bus that morning. Everybody else had their family and friends around them, but not me. It was hard to be positive and try to feel the joy of Christmas without my family.

The head Pastor welcomed everybody to the service, then other Pastors made some speeches and said some prayers. I cried quietly during this time. I was trying to be upbeat and happy and joyous like everybody else, but it was hard. It was a struggle to hide the fact that I was sad at such a happy gathering.

But I was missing my family, thinking about what it was like for us at Christmas and wondering what they would be doing now. Were there any presents for me? Christmas was very sad that year as I was reflecting on the Christmas times I'd had with my family and the traditions we have, waiting for everybody to wake up, sitting around the living room waiting for everybody to gather around, watching everybody open their presents. I really missed the joy and excitement of opening presents, the sounds of ripped paper flying off the presents, and watching my family receiving their presents.

At the church, we sang a couple Christian songs. Then we had Christmas lunch with all the trimmings - roast meat, roast vegetables and gravy.

There were a couple of speeches and then plum pudding.

I recall that when it was time to go to the kitchen to collect our plum pudding and dessert, a lady came up and spoke to me. She was in good spirits, polite, well-mannered and friendly.

"How are you?" she asked me.

I replied tearfully that I was not so good because I missed my family, and Christmas wasn't the same without them. At first the lady was shocked. She hugged me before our quick conversation was over. Out of all the people there, she was the only one I found to be sympathetic and empathic towards my situation. I had felt so isolated at my own table, and this was the one person with whom I connected the most through the whole time there. I know it was partly my fault for not interacting with the other people at the table, but I was also shy.

At about 2:30 in the afternoon I returned to the shared house where I lived.

At the time this experience taught me a lot and uplifted me. I learned to appreciate what you have and make the most of it, to be happy, to value, cherish and appreciate your family and friends no matter how much they drive you up the wall or send you bonkers. That Christmas service taught me all this. It reminded me to never forget that family, friends and your health are important and should always matter in your life.

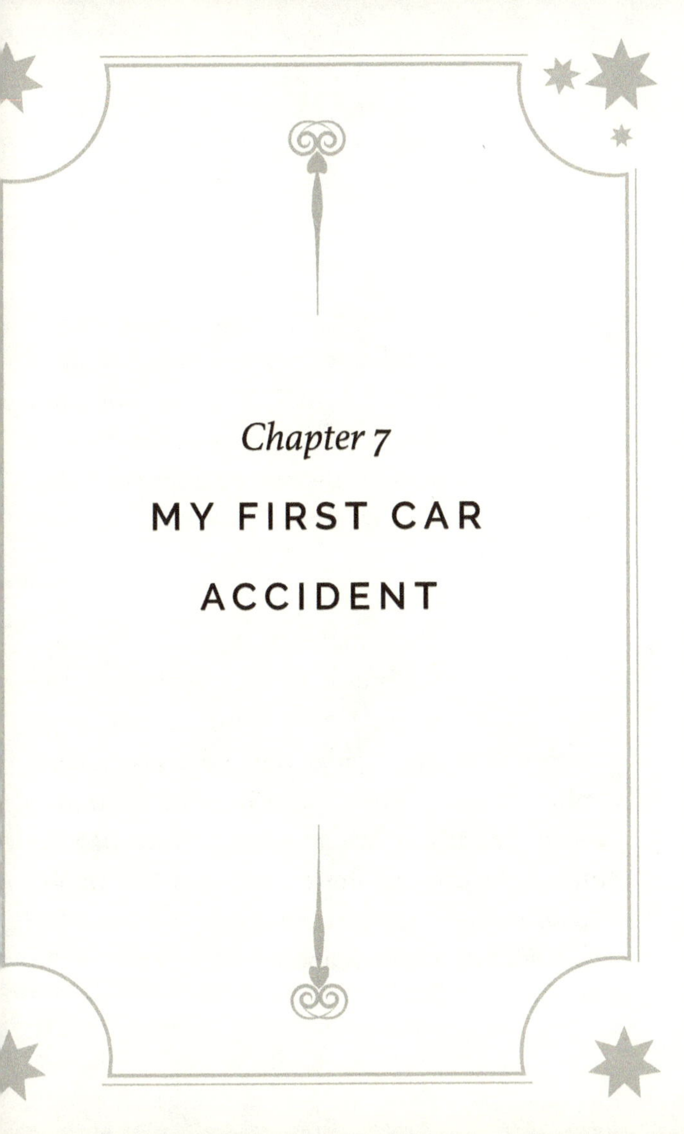

# Chapter 7

# MY FIRST CAR

# ACCIDENT

One day, in Melbourne, I was driving in my 1985 Toyota Corolla from the family home in Dandenong to my job in St Kilda on the outer fringe of the city. It was like any other drive to work, the same route, the same amount of traffic, and good driving weather. It was around 10:30 the morning.

I drove down the Princess Highway then turned onto Sir John Monash Drive; I arrived at the intersection where I always turned left to go under the railway bridge then take a right turn onto Normanby Road. At the intersection underneath the railway bridge, I had a green light to turn right around the corner into Normanby Road. As went to turn the corner I moved forward slightly, hesitant about moving around the corner. Then a car hit me from behind as it tried to follow behind me. I was turning through the intersection, but I stopped again as I was scared and in a bit of shock. My brain was thinking fast about how to get out of this situation, but I had just made it worse by stopping again!

At that moment a tram was coming from behind me in the left lane, ready  to turn the same corner as myself and the car behind me. In front of me in the right lane heading towards me was another car coming through the intersection, and at the intersection there was another tram in the right lane, also heading towards the intersection.

I continued around the corner and pulled over on the side of the road. The car that had hit me followed me, and we exchanged details, as we needed to because we had crashed. As we were doing so, the tram from the left lane behind us came past. No emergency services were called.

I wasn't lacking in confidence as I had been driving for a while, and I had taken this route many times. The difference was that I had been hesitating and asking myself whether I should or shouldn't proceed.

If I hadn't moved from the middle of the inter-section after my second moment of hesitation, there would have been a really nasty smash. The oncoming car in the right lane would have hit me on the left-hand side of my car near the front wheel. The car behind me would have hit me again, and the oncoming tram would also have hit both our cars if it hadn't been able to slow down in time. If this had happened, my car would have been a big smashed up mess with me trapped inside, as it was a small car and would have spun around from the impact of being hit.

Spiritually I had no indication, no intuitive feelings, clairvoyant visions, or anything like that at all to guide me, and warn me that something was about to go horribly wrong. That was my first car crash. Thankfully it was only minor, but it could have quite easily become a major accident which could have killed myself or others. I am so grateful that did not happen.

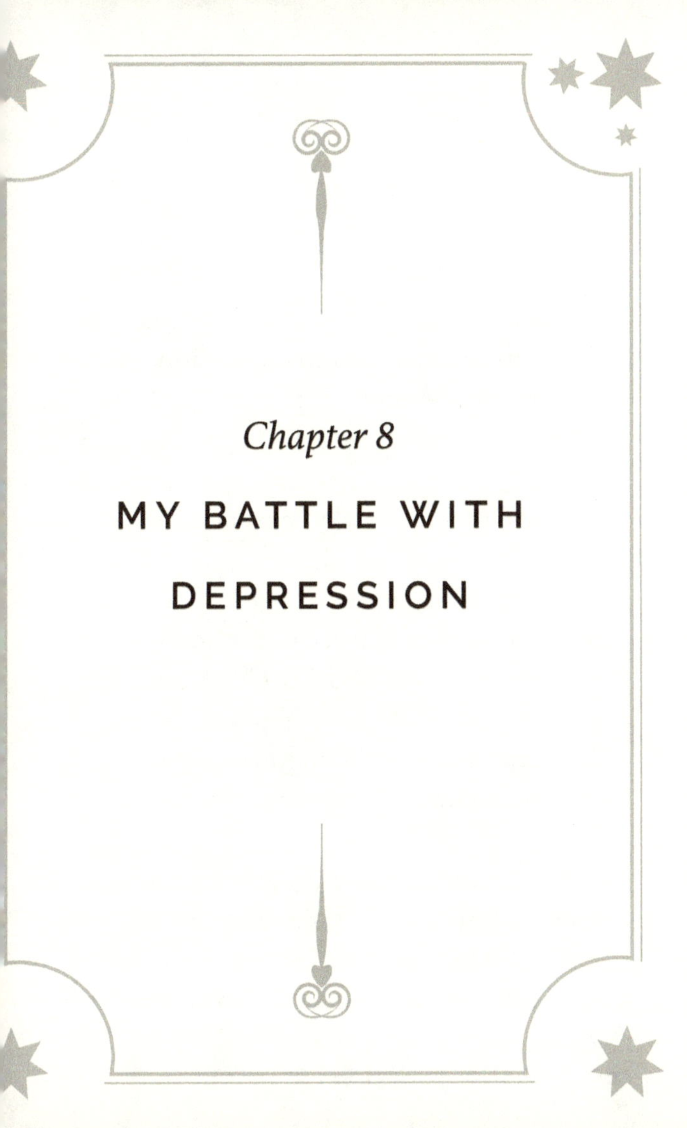

*Chapter 8*

# MY BATTLE WITH DEPRESSION

Towards the end of 2010, when I was 25 years old, I was diagnosed with depression. I was prescribed anti-depressants to assist me in battling the depression and help me to feel better.

It was a dark and "yucky" part of my life for two years. But in the end it was also positive and uplifting, because one day I had a light-bulb moment in which I decided to do something with my life. I realised I couldn't keep living a life in which I felt sad and spent my days feeling negative and thinking negative thoughts. I decided to change those negatives to a positive.

In 2011 I started a full-time job. Although at the time I wasn't overly excited or thrilled about it, it actually was a really positive experience to be offered this position. I was there for two years, which was great as up till then most of my employment experience had been seasonal.

This is when I started my affirmations and journalling. I would write down positives from my day into a journal, and from here on in my positive outlook began to grow. When I did have a depressing day, I would reflect back on my positives, then begin to feel uplifted, inspired again, grateful and motivated. It was a combination of the "little things" that seemed to make the most difference.

Every time I had a negative thought, I would choose to find or think of a happy thought to replace the negative. This all took time - a few months - but it worked well as a step-by-step process.

This was my breaking point, a breakthrough moment where I realised I just had to do something and make a change. And then there came a time when I thought I would stop taking the anti-depressants and just live my life by trying to be as positive as possible.

I don't suggest or recommend that you do the same as I did. I decided to stop taking medication to help and guide me through each day. It wasn't the best choice I could have made. I stopped my medication cold turkey, just like that, which can be dangerous.

I still remember telling my GP at the time. Believe me, it looked as if he was about to have a heart attack! But he asked lots of questions about my well-being and was surprised to hear my responses. At this point, I made the decision to totally change my life, and from then on my life has indeed changed in a positive way!

*Chapter 9*

# MY FIRST TAROT DECK

A while ago now, sometime in 2013, I bought a Rider Waite Tarot Deck. This was the moment of realisation for me. I noticed that something was calling me, giving me a sign that fortune telling of some kind was what I was meant to do, perhaps fortune telling with Tarot cards.

For a while, whenever I came home I would sit down in the lounge room and begin to use the Tarot cards. But then there were times when I would hide the cards and try to forget where they were, because I had developed a fear of the cards.

I was learning and interpreting what the cards meant, so I did readings for myself in order to get some practice and experience. I had no books to assist me in my learning, but now I know  that it would have been better if I had bought some books about tarot cards and the different spreads and so on.

So when I conducted readings for myself and made predictions with the cards, it was scary. More and more often, if I asked what next week would have in store for me, something from the reading turned out to be true and the predictions had a sense of accuracy about them.

This experience freaked me out because my knowledge and experience of Tarot was limited. I therefore made that decision not to use the tarot deck for a while, and I stopped for about two or three months. This was a brief but powerful experience, because it gave me a feeling inside that something had changed, and it was a part of my life. I had discovered that there was something special about myself and I had a unique quality!

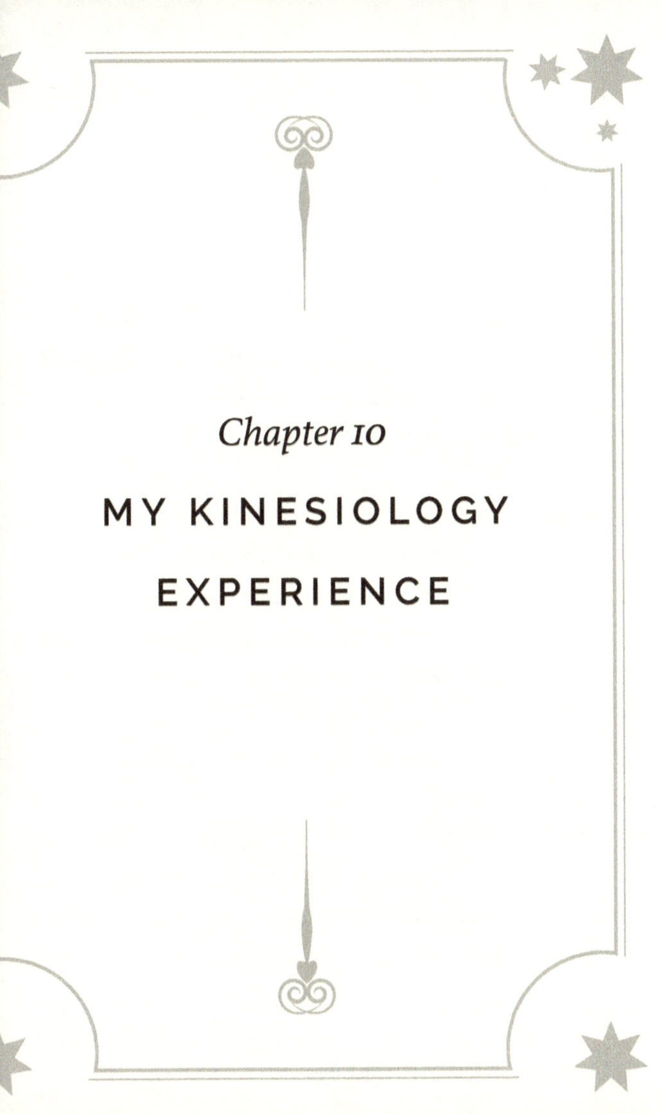

*Chapter 10*

# MY KINESIOLOGY

# EXPERIENCE

In 2013 I decided to get a bit of life experience and hopefully encounter something different. I had a few kinesiology sessions, and it was a very powerful experience.

It was powerful because I felt the process happening and changing within myself during the session when the kinesiologist spoke, telling me what he was doing and how he was doing it, and what I would feel or see, if anything at all.

It was a surreal experience for a first timer to kinesiology. Kinesiology is a mind, body, spiritual experience, something that I had never encountered before. I found that the relaxation therapy occurs all in one hit, and it restores and heals imbalances in your body. It works with the body's structural, chemical, emotional and any other energy.

Although this experience was positive and uplifting, it was also freaky for me as it was something I had never encountered before. As I listened to the kinesiologist and the instructions, I could feel internally what was happening. It was like a really long meditation session and felt to me almost like a medical intervention.

After the sessions I felt it had truly worked for me. I would be feeling light, uplifted and relaxed, and I experienced a sense of calm. Things that had been not quite right for me improved slightly but not dramatically, and my mood and thoughts became more positive as well. I haven't been back to have kinesiology since this occurrence, but I do recommend people giving it a try.

As for me, when I finally decided to experience kinesiology, my reason for going was to experience something different and try something new. When I had finished high school, back when I was living in Western Australia, I had aspired to be a kinesiologist. I had made lots of enquiries back then, and information arrived for me in the mail. I had to explain to my parents about what kinesiology was and tell them that I might want to study it, which was the reason that the letter box was occasionally full. But that was the day when I realised it wasn't for me.

*Chapter II*

# THAT COULD HAVE BEEN US!

This occurred back in 2014 at the private train-
ing college I was attending in the outer suburbs
of Melbourne.

One day at around 2 pm I started to not feel
right and was becoming agitated. The class finished at 2:30 and I insisted to my friend that I
needed to go to the toilet, then have a drink and
a chat about college stuff, study a bit more. I
just needed do something before she drove me
back to her house. I suggested things to her sev-
eral times prior to leaving.

At this time my intuition was telling me something wasn't right; my clairvoyance was showing me in my mind that something was going
to happening, that something was going to
hit something else. It was like having a movie

screen up on my forehead and seeing images or short videos flashing up on it. I was trying hard to figure out what was going to hit what, and what it could all mean.

Then we left the college and it was a normal drive back to my friend's house, just like it was on any other day that we went to college together. We were laughing, talking and chatting away about ourselves. We left Frankston CBD and decided to listen to music quietly in the background. Then we drove down Cranbourne Road, where the traffic was busy but not bad. It was the same route that we normally took.

We were about 30 minutes into our drive and nearly there, just another 15 to 20 minutes or so away. For a while the drive to my friend's place was like any other drive home, but then as we got closer the traffic started building up.

I said, "Something's not right, something's not right!" Yet again my intuition was telling me that something "wasn't right". My clairvoyance was showing me in my mind that something was going to happen, something was going to hit something else.

When we were another two kms down Cranbourne-Frankston Road, we saw a tow truck with a grey car on its tray. The car in front must have stopped suddenly and been hit by the car behind it. The oncoming grey car had its windscreen all smashed up!

At that moment my friend and I realised it could have been us. My friend was saying: "Oh gosh, that could have been us!" We could have been involved in the crash but we were lucky.

There was another experience to remind me I was still psychic and intuitive, and had another tale to tell. How lucky were we!

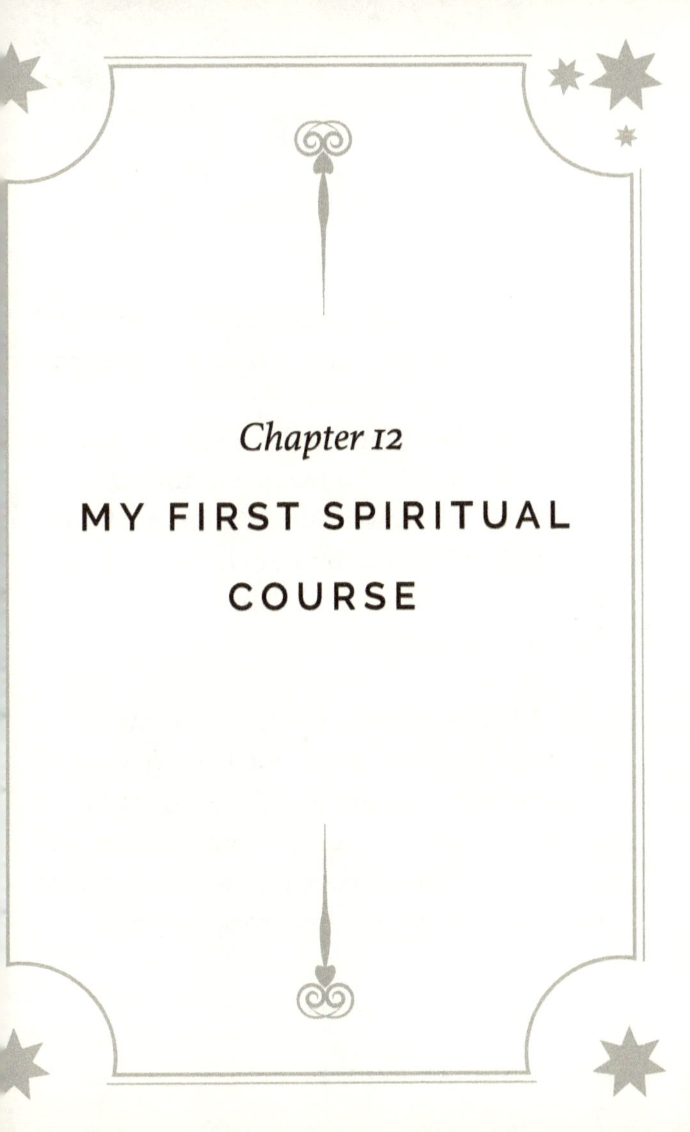

## Chapter 12

# MY FIRST SPIRITUAL COURSE

In 2016 I completed a course in Spirituality and then I made the decision to have a market stall.

I went to the Mind, Body, Spirit Festival in Melbourne and had a reading at the stall of a lovely lady who was visiting Melbourne for the festival. I had done a couple of laps around past all the stalls nearby, and then I came back to this particular stall.

After I had a reading, the lady told me about a course that she offers, but I didn't want to commit and sign up straight away. However, a couple months later I contacted her and enrolled into the course, called Ki Lao Ti, which was conducted via online correspondence.

So each week for seven weeks in a row I received a booklet of information and a weekly exercise. The course was designed to open yourself up spiritually and develop yourself in some way. Ki Lao Ti taught me Soul Therapy, Angelic Healing, Healing and Empowerment.

The journeying exercise helped me discover my own unique qualities, and put everything into perspective for me. It helped me to answer such questions as: this is why I have dreams at night, this is why I am intuitive, and so on. It also gave me a sense of empowerment.

I began to read spiritual books, and articles that I found on the internet by people like Louise Hay and Doreen Virtue. I really wanted to learn, and to understand how and why I feel this way, and how and why I know and sense the things that I do. I now have a small but growing collection of spiritual books.

I began to find the answers to some of the big questions of my life, such as:

*Why can't I stand being around negativity?*
*What do my dreams mean?*
*Why are some of them coming true?*

And when I looked at all the experiences from my past, I began to realise that everything happens for reason and there are no accidents. All the people who have come and gone in my life had something to teach and I was able to learn from them, or they learned something from me. It just made sense now. I had the feeling that "it just feels right", as if everything has came together as one.

I learned how to clear my own energies, and energies in my home and work. This was so beneficial for me because I often feel as if I have a heavy backpack strapped to me, and after a while I need to clear out those thoughts still buzzing around in my head, and I need to let go of those feelings tugging on my heartstrings again, triggering thoughts. I learned about letting go of things bothering me from last week or whenever, releasing and clearing it all from myself, and taking on the view that whatever will be, will be.

From here I made the decision to do something with my spiritual knowledge and experience.

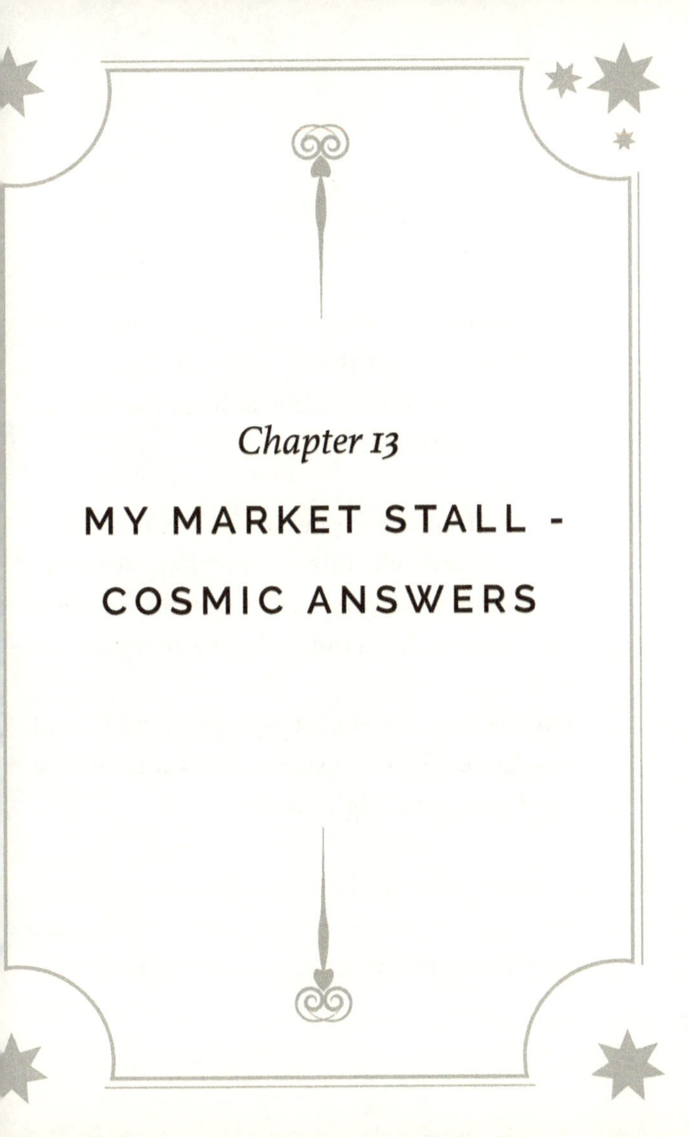

*Chapter 13*

# MY MARKET STALL - COSMIC ANSWERS

On the 11th of October 2016 I finally made the decision to "get out there" with my Tarot reading, and take it to the public at local markets so I could gain experience.

I thought of a name for my stall - *Cosmic Answers*. Cosmic means all things spiritual. Answers refers to the guidance, answers or information you are seeking from the cards or a reading.

When I set up my stall, I brought a table and chairs, table cloths, business cards and all the things I thought I might need.

The experience was both positive and negative. It was positive because I met some really awesome people, had awesome conversations with them, and got some good advice from them as well. I watched and listened in to other stall holders, and learned how they conducted themselves and their readings. I took on their advice if they offered me any that I could see would be of benefit to me in becoming a better stall holder and spiritual person.

I learned that reading people is both easy and hard. Some people want a reading but aren't easy to read because they won't open themselves to you. They are like a concrete wall. Some people would be great. They would give me heaps of information, could relate to me and their reading, and they would walk away from my stall feeling awesome. Delving into somebody's life is fascinating. You can hear, see and sense their experiences and life events that they've encountered. You sense their pain, heartache and emotions. All this was great experience to take on board, as I had never had a market stall before or done anything like this.

The negative side was that other stall holders had been doing it longer than me and had a bit more experience. My stall wasn't as vibrant as theirs. It was a bit dull and needed my personal touch and feel. Also, because I have a day job, my attendance was random and inconsistent according to my availability. But I still persisted and when I missed a market, I would attend the next one to see what the next experience would bring for me.

I offered small readings for about seven cards and then I would offer readings for an hour. I offered both for an affordable rate. I enjoyed reading for different people and getting intuitive "hits" and making "connections" from readings through the cards.

But then there came a time when I could sense that my stall wasn't doing well because of all the negatives, and I had to decide not to attend the market anymore. So from April 2017 I decided that rather than have my stall at the markets,

I would study more so I could learn and educate myself spiritually. I do plan to do it all again in the future. I feel determined and empowered to do it again with a bang and a bit of a "wow" factor. But I trust that whatever will be, will be.

*Chapter 14*

# BEDTIME PRAYER

Some days are good and some are bad, and some days are just horrible. Work, school, university, family, friends - all these things can keep us busy throughout our day. At night I have a routine, and this routine helps to relax and calm my mind. Sometimes it is hard to stick to the routine. Sometimes I miss or forget some part of my routine. And then there are some things I just don't forget to do!

My night-time routine consists of a few things before going to sleep, things that are quick and easy. They help my body and mind to wind down and know that it's time for bed. I brush my teeth (sometimes I forget!), I journal, and sometimes I write a to-do list so I don't stress about tomorrow before tomorrow has even arrived.

I found that, depending on the day, it can be easy to unwind and relax from the day, or sometimes it's just a struggle. I began to wonder what would help me to unwind and relax and get a good night's sleep, ready for the day ahead.

And then one day I decided to write a little prayer to say before going to sleep at night. I wrote down all those I wished to pray for or would like to help, and found it aided well and allowed me to rest a little better. After a while this prayer below was created:

> *Dear Angels,*
> *Now as I lay down to rest*
> *Today I've done my best*
> *Angels watch over me as I sleep*
> *As I relax my body and calm my mind*
> *Protect me with divine love and light*
> *Then wake me up in the morning light.*
>
> *Thank you.*

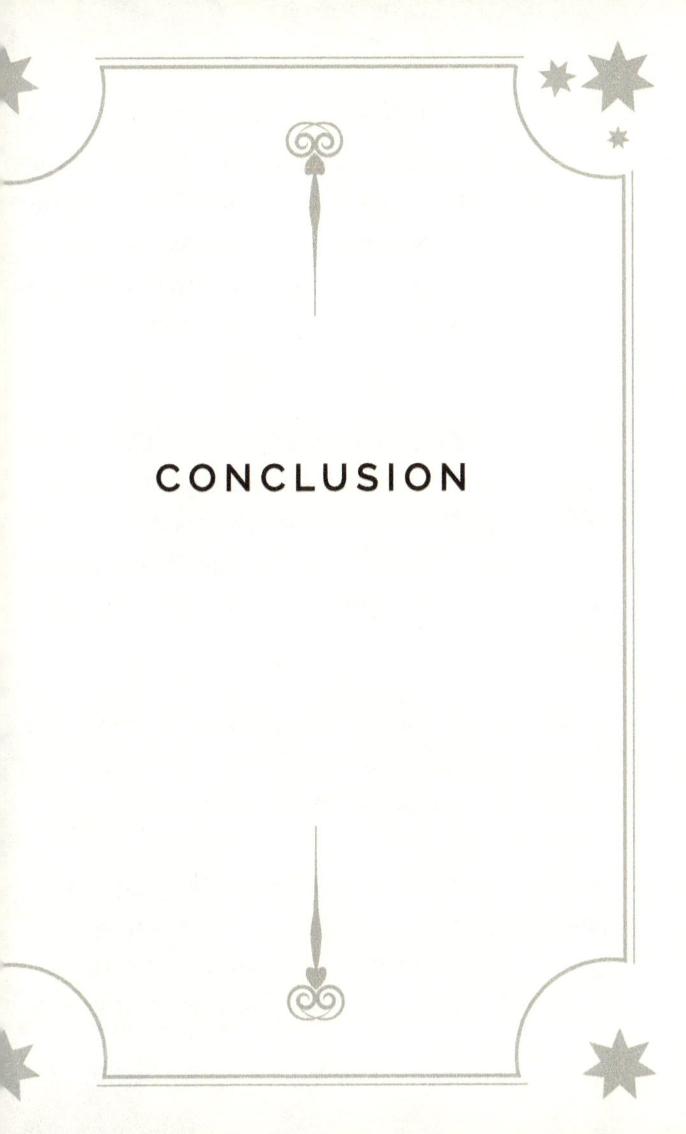

# CONCLUSION

This is something I have wanted to do for a little while now. I have wanted to share my experiences with people. I have wanted to share my inspiration, and entertain and inspire people through my stories. I have encountered all this in a spiritual sense, and written every little bit that I could possibly recall, recite and remember.

What's next for me? I plan to go back to reading at markets. I plan to set up my Oracle Card Reading stall *Cosmic Answers* again. Soon I will be offering my readings, meeting new clients, and all those awesome things about being at the markets!

There are also a few other things I would like to do, but I am keeping them a secret for now. Maybe I might just write another book?

To my followers on my Facebook page *Cosmic Answers*: you have seen me progress, change and grow on this journey, and you have liked, commented and shared what I've put on my page.

You have always liked it when I posted photos of my cards. That seems to be the highlight of my page for you. So thank you to all those who have followed my journey online.

For those reading this book, I hope it has inspired you, and thank you for reading!

# REFERENCES

## CHAPTER 4

http://www.traveller.com.au/south-australia-haunted-tours-8-haunting-experiences-that-will-scare-you-gpiine

https://www.behindthename.com/names/description/nona

*Please share my experiences.*